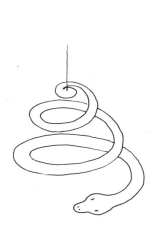

Colour these snakes in bright
colours and then cut along the
spiral to the centre.
Sew a thread into the tail to
make a mobile or...

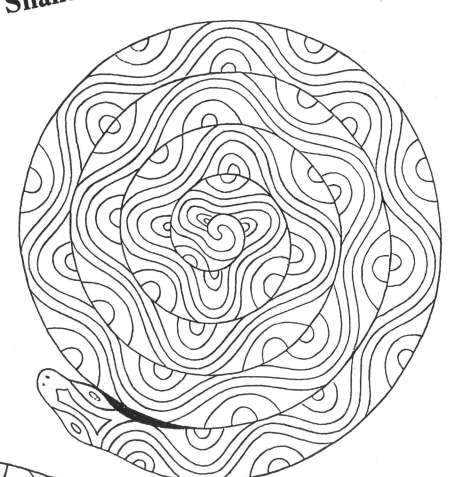

...make a cone from coloured
paper and rest the snake's tail
on the point.

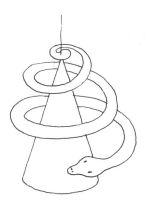

1

Paper Presents... Paper Presents... Paper Presents

Bookmarks... Bookmarks... Bookmarks

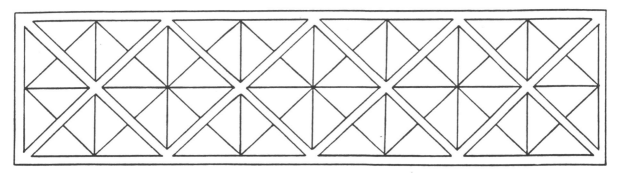

Five lovely bookmarks to colour, cut out and give away as a special gift.
Make sure that the people you give them to never lose their places in a book ever again!

This large table mat is a delight to colour as the pattern weaves under and over itself.
It can be a very special present for someone living on their own,
or you could trace or photocopy the design on to card and make as many mats as you wish.

Treasure box... Treasure box... Treasure box

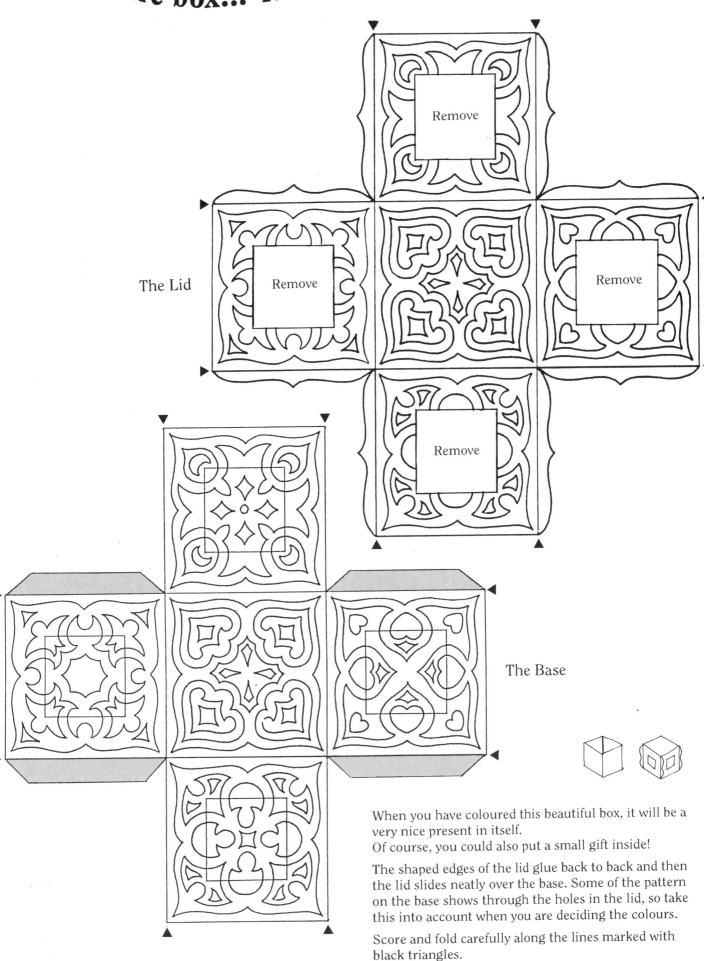

The Lid

Remove

Remove

Remove

Remove

The Base

When you have coloured this beautiful box, it will be a very nice present in itself.
Of course, you could also put a small gift inside!

The shaped edges of the lid glue back to back and then the lid slides neatly over the base. Some of the pattern on the base shows through the holes in the lid, so take this into account when you are deciding the colours.

Score and fold carefully along the lines marked with black triangles.

Remove Remove

Remove Remove

Remove Remove

Colour and cut out these three masks and use them for a party. Don't forget to cut out the eye-holes!
Hold the masks in place with a piece of thin elastic or string around the back of your head.
The black dots show the best places to make the holes.

You have plenty of choice on how to colour these coasters, as there are six different designs to work on.
When you have finished colouring them, cut them out and give them to someone as a present to protect a table from drips from glasses or cups. If you have any thin self-adhesive plastic film available, try covering the coasters with it . If you can make them waterproof, both they and the table will be better protected!

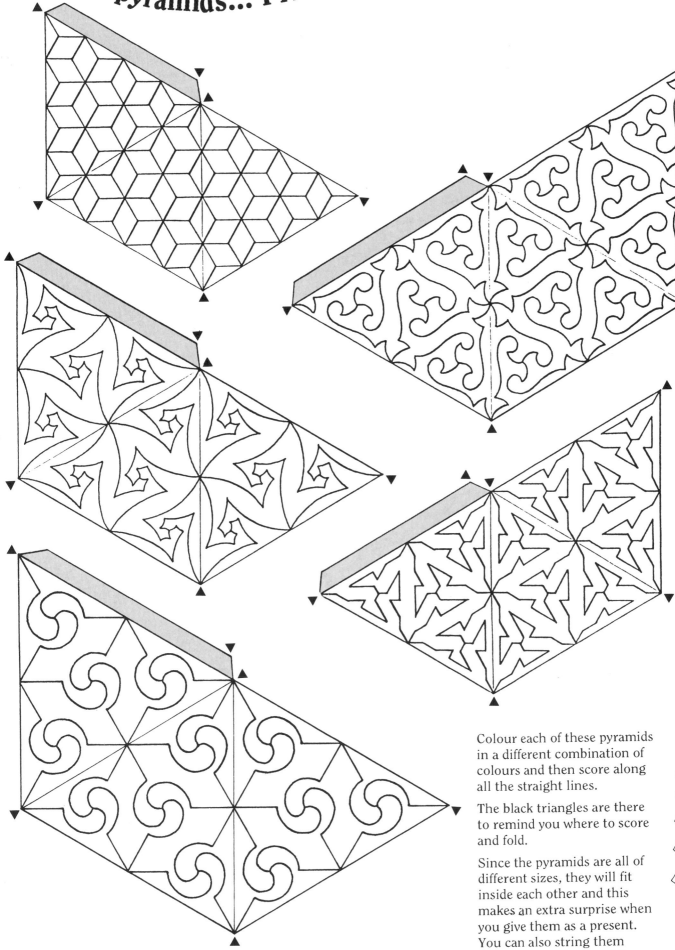

Colour each of these pyramids in a different combination of colours and then score along all the straight lines.

The black triangles are there to remind you where to score and fold.

Since the pyramids are all of different sizes, they will fit inside each other and this makes an extra surprise when you give them as a present. You can also string them together to make a mobile.

Colour these five cards and send them to friends and relatives. Three fold in half and two are flat.

*Best
Wishes*

*Best
Wishes*

*Best
Wishes*

*Best
Wishes*

*Best
Wishes*

These are called 'arabesque mats because the designs are mostly made up of curves and scrolls. Notice that the individual pieces of each pattern occurs eight times and so you will find them very pleasing to colour if you use four different shades.

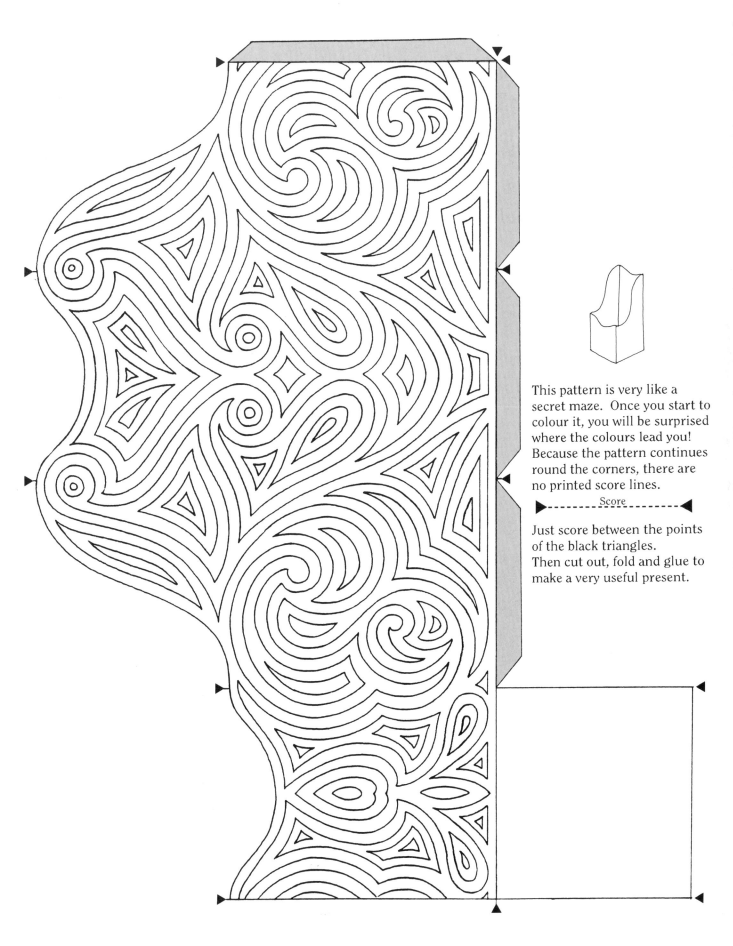

This pattern is very like a secret maze. Once you start to colour it, you will be surprised where the colours lead you! Because the pattern continues round the corners, there are no printed score lines.

◀------- Score -------◀

Just score between the points of the black triangles.
Then cut out, fold and glue to make a very useful present.

After you have coloured these charming paper dolls, cut them out and glue the skirts to make cone shapes.
They are all different sizes, so they fit inside each other, just like those amazing sets of Russian dolls.
A delightful present for someone!

Napkin rings... Napkin rings... Napkin rings

Colour these strips and make a set of napkin rings for a special occasion. This paper on its own is probably not strong enough to use more than once, so it is a good idea to glue your strips to some thicker card. Don't worry if you overlap it by more than the grey area as long as the napkin will still fit inside!

23

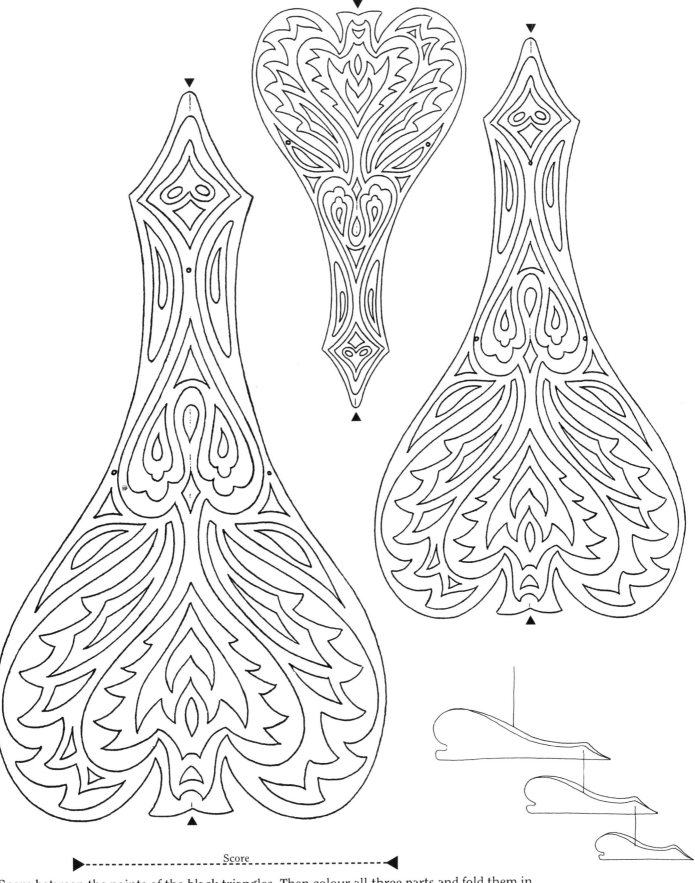

Score

Score between the points of the black triangles. Then colour all three parts and fold them in half so that the patterns are on the outside and the grey on the inside. Then make a mobile.

Square bookmarks... Square bookmarks

These bookmarks fit neatly over the corner of a page and remain firmly in place until the reader wants to continue.
When you have coloured each bookmark, cut it out, fold and glue the grey tabs.
The black triangles remind you where to score and fold. And don't forget to colour the larger triangles too!

Paper Presents... Paper Presents... Paper Presents

Dodecoration... Dodecoration... Dodecoration

This paper present is in the form of a beautiful mathematical shape called a dodecahedron. Its name comes from the Greek words which mean 'twelve sides'.

When you have 'dodecorated' it, score along all the straight lines. Then fold and crease firmly and it will be quite clear how the model glues together.

Zig-zag cards... Zig-zag cards... Zig-zag cards

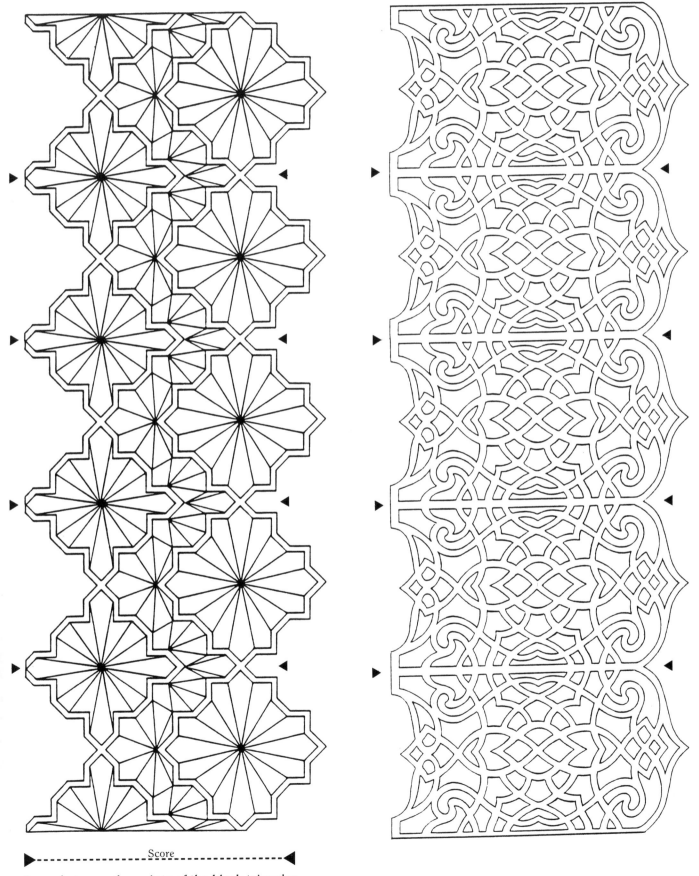

▶------------------- Score -------------------◀

Score between the points of the black triangles.
When you have coloured each of the cards, fold them into a zig-zag and write a suitable greeting on the back.